The Midwest

DANA MEACHEN RAU

Children's Press®
An Imprint of Scholastic Inc.
New York Toronto London Auckland Sydney
Mexico City New Delhi Hong Kong
Danbury, Connecticut

Front cover, center: Gateway Arch in St. Louis, Missouri
Front cover, top right: Mount Rushmore in South Dakota
Front cover, bottom left: Chicago River in Chicago, Illinois

Content Consultant
James Wolfinger, PhD
Associate Professor
DePaul University
Chicago, Illinois

Library of Congress Cataloging-in-Publication Data

Rau, Dana Meachen, 1971–
   The Midwest/by Dana Meachen Rau.
      p. cm. — (A true book)
   Includes bibliographical references and index.
   ISBN-13: 978-0-531-24850-8 (lib. bdg.)   ISBN-10: 0-531-24850-X (lib. bdg.)
   ISBN-13: 978-0-531-28325-7 (pbk.)   ISBN-10: 0-531-28325-9 (pbk.)
   1. Middle West—Juvenile literature. I. Title.
   F351.R38 2012
   977—dc23   2011031389

All rights reserved. Published in 2012 by Children's Press, an imprint of Scholastic Inc.
Printed in China 62
SCHOLASTIC, CHILDREN'S PRESS, A TRUE BOOK, and associated logos are trademarks and/or registered trademarks of Scholastic Inc.
1 2 3 4 5 6 7 8 9 10 R 21 20 19 18 17 16 15 14 13 12

Find the Truth!

Everything you are about to read is true *except* for one of the sentences on this page.

Which one is **TRUE**?

T or F All of the Midwestern states border the Great Lakes.

T or F All top-10 corn-producing states in the United States are in the Midwest.

Find the answers in this book.

3

Contents

Western meadowlark

Dairy farms are a common sight in Wisconsin.

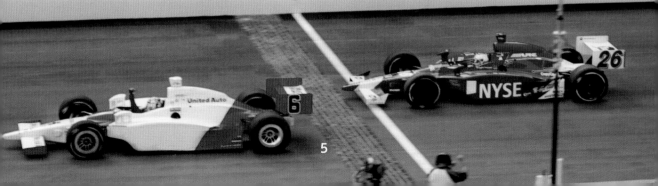

4 Resources and Economy

How does the Midwest make use of its resources? **31**

5 Feeding the Nation

What challenges does the Midwest face? **39**

The oval track at the Indianapolis Motor Speedway is 2.5 miles (4 km) long.

CANADA

Missouri R.

GREAT

NORTH DAKOTA

⊗ Bismarck   ● Fargo

Superior
Uplands

Lake Superior

Great Lakes

MINNESOTA

MICHIGAN

Lake Huron

Lake Ontari

SOUTH DAKOTA

⊗ Pierre

Minneapolis ● ⊗ St.Paul

WISCONSIN

Black
Hills

● Sioux Falls

Madison
⊗

● Milwaukee

Lansing
⊗

Lake Michigan

Detroit ●

Lake Erie

Mississippi R.

Corn Belt

IOWA

Chicago ●

Canton ●

NEBRASKA

Missouri R.

Des Moines ●

OHIO

● Omaha
Lincoln ⊗

ILLINOIS

INDIANA

Columbus ●

Springfield
⊗

Indianapolis
⊗

Ohio R.

Kansas City ●

Topeka ⊗

Jefferson City ⊗   ● St. Louis

P L A I N S

KANSAS

MISSOURI

St. Francois
Mountains

Appalachian Mountains

● Wichita

Ozark
Mountains

Mississippi River

MEXICO

Gulf of Mexico

The United States

0   miles   200

0   km   200

N
W ⊗ E
S

Middle of the Nation

The Midwest region includes 12 states. They are Illinois, Indiana, Iowa, Kansas, Michigan, Minnesota, Missouri, Nebraska, North Dakota, Ohio, South Dakota, and Wisconsin. To the east, south, and west, the Midwest is surrounded by other U.S. states. In the north, it shares a border with Canada. Half of the midwestern states have shores on the Great Lakes.

The Great Lakes together are the largest area of freshwater on Earth.

Look at the Land

The Great Plains are called "great" for a reason. This high area of dry, grassy land is huge. It starts in northern Canada and stretches down all the way to Texas. The Great Plains cover parts of North Dakota, South Dakota, Nebraska, and Kansas.

The Till Plains lie to the east of the Great Plains. Thousands of years ago, glaciers carved out this land. The glaciers left behind a **fertile** type of soil called till.

Plains stretch as far as the eye can see in much of the Midwest.

The Black Hills are a popular tourist spot.

The Midwest lies between the United States' two main mountain ranges. To the east are the Appalachians. To the west are the Rockies. But the Midwest itself has some high areas, too. The Superior Uplands of Minnesota are rugged. There are the Black Hills in South Dakota and the St. Francois Mountains of Missouri. The land also rises into a high **plateau** in eastern Ohio near the Appalachians.

The Missouri is the longest U.S. river.

Waters of the Midwest

The two longest rivers in the United States flow through the Midwest. The Missouri River starts in Montana and flows down through the state of Missouri. Near St. Louis, it meets the Mississippi River, which flows from Minnesota to the Gulf of Mexico. Both rivers have served as important **waterways** and water sources for the region. Many people have settled near the rivers for this reason.

The Great Lakes are also important bodies of water. They were carved out by glaciers millions of years ago. Fishers have long depended on the lakes for their fish. The lakes are connected to each other, and the St. Lawrence Seaway joins them all to the Atlantic Ocean. This makes it easy to ship goods back and forth. Industries have sprouted up around the lakes to take advantage of the waterway.

Many of the largest cities in the Midwest, such as Cleveland, Ohio, are located near the Great Lakes.

Climate

The Midwest has a humid **continental climate**. There is a big difference between summer and winter. In summer, the hot sun beats overhead. **Precipitation** falls as rain. Winters can be bitterly cold. Snow may cover the ground all season long. Schools sometimes close for a time when the weather is very bad. The trip to school can be dangerous in heavy snow and ice. Teachers and students stay safe at home.

Powerful snowstorms are common across the Midwest.

12

Tornadoes cause massive damage to homes and businesses.

The Midwest experiences many severe storms. Cold air from Canada and the northwestern states blows south over the flat plains. It runs into warm, moist air from the Gulf of Mexico drifting north. The two swirl around, trying to balance each other. Blizzards, hail, and thunderstorms develop. So do tornadoes. Most tornadoes occur in an area called Tornado Alley, between the Rocky Mountains and the Appalachian Mountains. People here often build storm shelters underground. Inside, people are safe until the storm passes.

Bison were once common throughout the Great Plains.

CHAPTER 2

History of the Midwest

Before European settlers arrived, many Native American nations lived on the grasslands of the Great Plains. They included the Crow, Sioux, Cheyenne, and Pawnee. Some people farmed the land, growing corn, wheat, and other crops. Others gathered food. They also hunted the huge bison herds that roamed the grasslands.

 Native Americans used bison hide to make warm winter clothing and shoes.

Fighting Over Land

In the late 1600s, the French settled areas around the Great Lakes. The region was full of beavers and other animals. Settlers could become wealthy selling the animals' valuable skins in Europe. There, they were made into clothing.

In 1682, French explorer René-Robert Cavelier, Sieur de La Salle, followed the Mississippi River. He claimed its valley for France and named it Louisiana. The French protected their claim by building forts. They made **alliances** with Native Americans.

La Salle quickly recognized the importance of the Mississippi River.

Both the French and the British had alliances with different Native American groups.

The French and Indian War gave Great Britain control over much of North America.

The French needed their forts and alliances. Britain had settled America east of the Appalachian Mountains. Britain wanted France's valuable land. The two countries fought from 1754 to 1763. Britain eventually won all the French lands east of the Mississippi River.

The United States became its own nation in 1783, after the Revolutionary War with Britain. The United States doubled in size in 1803 by purchasing the Louisiana Territory from France, gaining access to the present-day Midwest.

Eager to Expand

Pioneers headed westward to settle the new lands. Thousands poured into what was called the Northwest Territory. The territory included today's midwestern states east of the Mississippi. Native Americans battled these settlers. They wanted to keep their land.

Settlers also headed toward California. They started in Missouri and crossed the plains in covered wagons. They followed routes such as the Oregon Trail. In the late 1800s, railroads connecting the East to the West made travel safer and faster.

Midwestern Timeline

1682
La Salle of France claims the Mississippi River valley for France.

1754–1763
England and France fight over land in North America.

Land for Farmers

In 1862, the U.S. government wanted more people to move into the Midwest. They passed the Homestead Act, which gave land to farmers. Some pioneers seeking land came from the eastern states. African Americans came from the South. They wanted a new life after being freed from slavery following the Civil War. **Immigrants** came from Norway, Germany, Russia, and many other countries. They built sod houses and set up schools and churches where their communities could gather.

1841–1860
The Oregon Trail, starting in Missouri, serves as a main route west.

1803
The United States purchases the Louisiana Territory from France.

1862
The Homestead Act gives government land to small farmers.

Small farms grew into large ones. But farming life was not easy. Summers were very hot and often brought tornadoes. Winters were extremely cold and brought blizzards. Improvements in farming methods, such as better plows and harvesting machines, soon helped grain crops thrive. Railroads, shipping ports, and other industries helped farmers share their goods with the rest of the United States. The Midwest became known as the Breadbasket of America.

Many railroads were constructed throughout the 1800s.

Artists and Inventors of the Midwest

Langston Hughes (1902–1967) (right) was a poet, novelist, playwright, and newspaper columnist. He is best known for writing about African American life. He was born in Missouri and grew up in Ohio.

Langston Hughes

Walt Disney (1901–1966) was an animator who created such famous characters as Mickey Mouse and Donald Duck. He was born in Illinois.

Wilbur (1867–1912) and **Orville** (1871–1948) **Wright** invented the first practical airplane. The brothers grew up in Ohio and performed many of their experiments there.

Michael Jackson (1958–2009) was a singer, songwriter, and dancer whose success earned him the nickname the King of Pop. He was born in Indiana.

Large Midwestern cities such as Detroit, Michigan, are home to millions of people.

CHAPTER 3

People of the Midwest

The Midwest includes some of the largest cities and smallest towns in the United States. To the east, cities thrive around the Great Lakes. Other cities sprouted up along the region's major rivers.

Further west, the population is thinly spread. The U.S. government divided up much of this land over the years. Farmers grow crops on land once granted by the Homestead Act. Native groups live on land fought for by their ancestors and now protected by the government.

The Gateway Arch is a popular tourist attraction.

In the Cities

St. Louis, Missouri, is called the Gateway to the West. It is an important crossroads between east and west. The city lies on the Mississippi River, near where the Mississippi meets the Missouri. The rivers provide boats with access to other parts of the country. The city's airport, railroads, and highways also bring people and goods through as they travel across the nation. The city shares its nickname with the Gateway Arch. It towers 630 feet (192 meters) into the sky.

The location of Chicago, Illinois, on Lake Michigan makes it an important port. As a result, many industries have been built around it. Immigrants from Europe and African Americans from the South moved to Chicago in the 1800s and 1900s to work. Many of their **descendants** still live in the city. Immigrants from Asia, the Americas, and other places continue to arrive today. Their mix of cultures can be seen in the city's many neighborhoods.

Just under three million people live in Chicago.

On the Farms

People are more spread out in the western parts
of the Midwest. American settlers first came here
to take advantage of the Homestead Act. Farmers
have stayed in the region because of its rich soil.
Farms can cover many acres. Because of this,
people often live far away from each other. Small
towns are scattered across the farmland. People
gather there for supplies, yearly festivals, or just to
catch up with each other.

**Farms large and small are spread throughout
the Midwest.**

From above,
midwestern
farmland
looks like a
patchwork quilt.

Native Americans, such as the Cheyenne River Sioux in South Dakota, still celebrate the traditions of their ancestors.

Native Americans in the Midwest

Native American groups lived in the Midwest long before European or American settlers came. American settlers and the U.S. Army forced some of them out, such as the Pawnee. Other groups, including many Sioux tribes, live in the region today. Many of them live on reservations. Some of the largest **reservations** are in South Dakota. Tribes practice their customs through crafts, language, and celebrations. Powwows are colorful gatherings that include traditional clothing, dancing, and music.

Animals of the
Midwest

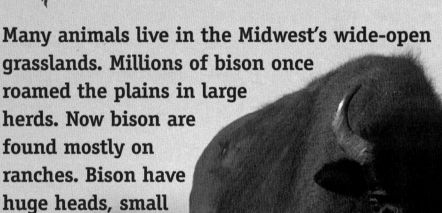

Many animals live in the Midwest's wide-open grasslands. Millions of bison once roamed the plains in large herds. Now bison are found mostly on ranches. Bison have huge heads, small horns, and long, shaggy fur. They graze on grasses and shrubs.

Black-tailed prairie dogs are small mammals. Their underground burrows have many tunnels and rooms. These "towns" house hundreds of prairie dogs. The animals are always on the lookout and will call to warn each other if danger is near.

Western meadowlarks are the state bird of three midwestern states: Kansas, Nebraska, and North Dakota. These yellow songbirds feed on insects and often perch on fence posts to sing.

Sunflowers are one of the most colorful crops grown in the Midwest.

CHAPTER 4

Resources and Economy

The Midwest produces many of the things people use and consume every day. The region's cars, motorcycles, and aircraft take people where they need to go. Its farms and factories produce much of the food in home refrigerators and cabinets. Its shipping docks, railroads, and airports send the products around the country and the world.

 Kansas's nickname is the Sunflower State.

Corn is used in a wide variety of products.

Iowa grows more corn than any other state.

Farms

The one thing that keeps most of the Midwest's economy running is the region's farmland. The seasonal weather and rich soil of the Midwest make it the perfect place for corn to grow. In fact, it is one of the most abundant corn-producing areas in the world. The main area of the Corn Belt is part of almost every state in the Midwest. The United States' top 10 corn-producing states are all in this region.

The Corn Belt is not the only midwestern farmland that features a particular product. The Dairy Belt passes through Wisconsin, Minnesota, and Michigan. Here, dairy cows feed on prairie grasslands. Their milk is used to make cheese, butter, and milk.

The Wheat Belt cuts through Kansas, Nebraska, and the Dakotas. Wheat is grown to make flour for bread, pasta, and other grain foods.

There are thousands of dairy farms in the Midwest.

Food Processing

Many factories of the Midwest process the foods grown and raised in the region. Mills in Kansas grind wheat into flour. Factories make breads, pastas, baked goods, and breakfast cereals. Corn is processed into corn oil, corn syrup, and popcorn. Corn is also used to feed animals.

At food-processing plants, milk is turned into butter, cheese, yogurt, and ice cream. Other factories produce frozen or canned foods. The region has many meatpacking plants, too.

Huge amounts of corn and other crops must be processed before they are useful.

Henry Ford invented the assembly line to speed the production of automobiles.

Other Industries

The automotive industry is centered in Detroit, Michigan. Its many car and truck factories have earned it the nickname Motor City.

In 2008 and 2009, the U.S. economy collapsed. Many car companies lost money. Detroit's General Motors and Chrysler were two of the hardest hit. Factories closed down, and many people lost their jobs. Since then, recovery has been slow. Jobs remain difficult to find, but companies and organizations are working to bring jobs back to the city.

Each year about 400,000 fans pack the Indianapolis Motor Speedway to watch the Indianapolis 500.

Tourism is a major industry across the Midwest. Tourists visit the Indianapolis Motor Speedway in Indiana. They watch cars race around the track at the Indianapolis 500. In Indianola, Iowa, tourists watch hot air balloons float through the sky during the summer's National Balloon Classic. Other people travel to Minnesota and the Dakotas to hike and ski in the area's mountains. Tourists spend money on hotels, restaurants, and other businesses. These businesses provide jobs for the towns' residents.

Football Hall of Fame

American football is one of the most popular sports in the United States. Canton, Ohio, is home to the Pro Football Hall of Fame. Visitors come to see exhibits about the game and its players. Many of the players included come from midwestern teams. The Green Bay Packers of Wisconsin have several players in the Hall of Fame. So do the Cleveland Browns, Chicago Bears, and St. Louis Rams.

Farmers' markets are a popular way for midwestern farmers to sell their crops.

CHAPTER 5

Feeding the Nation

Fields of strong healthy crops are a common sight in the Midwest. But farmers in this region have had to **adapt** to meet challenges caused by the weather.

One challenge with the weather in the Midwest is drought. Plants need sunlight, soil, and water to grow. The Midwest gets plenty of sunlight. But sometimes rain doesn't fall. A long period of time with no rainfall is called a drought.

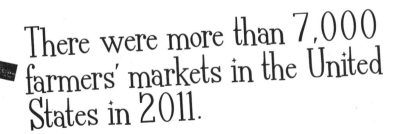

There were more than 7,000 farmers' markets in the United States in 2011.

Droughts Can Hurt Everyone

Long, hot summers without enough rain can cause crops and animals to die. When there are fewer crops, food prices go up. That means people must pay more money for food at the supermarket. When farmers do not have as many crops to sell, other industries are hurt too. Factories do not sell as much farm machinery because farmers can't afford to buy the new machines. Midwestern food processing factories must cut back on production or buy food at higher prices.

Droughts can cause major problems for farmers and the people who use their crops.

Farmers continue to use new technology to keep their crops and land healthy.

Dealing With Droughts

Farmers can reduce the effects of drought. One way is to use irrigation. This is a mechanical system for bringing water to crops. Today's farmers also use modern computers with their irrigation systems. The computers can help the farmer be sure the plants are getting enough water to grow. But the computer also makes sure that the plants are not getting more water than they need. This helps farmers use less water.

Farmers harvest their crops in late summer and through the fall.

Farming brings many challenges to the Midwest. But farmers work hard to keep their crops growing in all conditions. They know that many people depend on them. The food grown in the Midwest feeds more than just the people of the region. It feeds the people of the United States and the world. ★

True Statistics

Number of states in the region: 12

Major rivers of the region: Ohio, Mississippi, Missouri

Major mountain ranges of the region: Ozarks

Climate: Humid continental, semiarid

Largest cities: Chicago, IL; Indianapolis, IN; Columbus, OH

Products: Corn, wheat, and other grains; fruits; vegetables; livestock; coal; lumber; oil; natural gas

Borders of the region:

North: Canada

East: Northeast region

South: Southeast region

West: West region

Did you find the truth?

F All of the midwestern states border the Great Lakes.

T All top-10 corn-producing states in the United States are in the Midwest.

Resources

Books

King, David C. *The Sioux*. New York: Marshall Cavendish Benchmark, 2006.

Kummer, Patricia K. *The Great Lakes*. New York: Marshall Cavendish Benchmark, 2009.

Marrin, Albert. *Years of Dust: The Story of the Dust Bowl*. New York: Dutton Children's Books, 2009.

McNeese, Tim. *The Missouri River*. Philadelphia: Chelsea House Publishers, 2004.

Micucci, Charles. *The Life and Times of Corn*. Boston: Houghton Mifflin Books for Children, 2009.

Perritano, John. *The Lewis and Clark Expedition*. New York: Children's Press, 2010.

Rau, Dana Meachen. *North America*. Chanhassen, MN: The Child's World, 2004.

Rebman, Renee C. *How Do Tornadoes Form?* New York: Marshall Cavendish Benchmark, 2011.

Santella, Andrew. *The French and Indian War*. Minneapolis, MN: Compass Point Books, 2004.

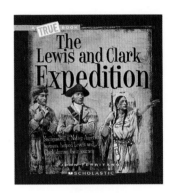

Web Sites

Smithsonian National Museum of American History
http://americanhistory.si.edu
Check out this site to see exhibits and learn about the growth of America.

U.S. Census 2010 Interactive Population Map
http://2010.census.gov/2010census/popmap
Learn about the populations of the states with this interactive map.

Places to Visit

The Gateway Arch
707 North First Street
St. Louis, MO 63102
(877) 982-1410
www.gatewayarch.com
Visit the tallest national monument in the United States, take a ride up to the top, or visit the Museum of Westward Expansion to learn about how the United States grew as a nation.

The Henry Ford Museum
20900 Oakwood Boulevard
Dearborn, MI 48124-5029
(313) 982-6001
www.thehenryford.org/index. aspx
Explore the inventions and ideas that helped shape America, and walk into the past on a tour of Greenfield Village.

 Visit this Scholastic web site for more information on the U.S. Midwest:
www.factsfornow.scholastic.com

Important Words

adapt (uh-DAPT) — to change because you are in a different situation

alliances (uh-LYE-uhns-ez) — agreements to work together for some result

continental climate (KAHN-tuh-nuhnt-uhl KLYE-mit) — the weather typical of a place over a long period of time that has annual temperature variations because of the lack of nearby large bodies of water

descendants (dih-SEN-duhnts) — a person's children, their children, and so on into the future

fertile (FUR-tuhl) — land that is good for growing crops and plants

immigrants (IM-i-gruhntz) — people who come from abroad to live permanently in a country

plateau (pla-TOH) — area of high, flat land

precipitation (pri-sip-i-TAY-shuhn) — the falling of water from the sky in the form of rain, sleet, hail, or snow

reservations (rez-ur-VAY-shuhnz) — areas of land set aside by the government for a special purpose

waterways (WAW-tur-wayz) — rivers, canals, or other bodies of water on which ships and boats can travel

Index

Page numbers in **bold** indicate illustrations

About the Author

Dana Meachen Rau is the author of more than 300 books for children. A graduate of Trinity College in Hartford, Connecticut, she has written fiction and nonfiction titles including early readers and books on science, history, cooking, and many other topics that interest her. She especially loves to write books that take her to other places, even when she doesn't have time for a vacation. Dana lives with her family in Burlington, Connecticut. To learn more about her books, please visit *www.danameachenrau.com*.